Miyabi

5 JAPANESE IMPRESSIONS FOR PIANO SOLO

by Naoko Ikeda

Miyabi 雅 *is a traditional Japanese aesthetic ideal meaning "refinement" or "elegance."*

ISBN 978-1-4584-2492-1

WILLIS MUSIC

EXCLUSIVELY DISTRIBUTED BY

HAL•LEONARD®
CORPORATION

7777 W. BLUEMOUND RD. P.O. BOX 13819 MILWAUKEE, WI 53213

Visit Hal Leonard Online at
www.halleonard.com

CONTENTS

3 .... RAFT OF FLOWERS

6 .... PLUM BLOSSOMS

9 .... PEONIES

12 .... AOI

14 .... SOFT RAIN

PERFORMANCE NOTES

Miyabi was inspired by the beauty of flowers that bloom from spring to early summer. These five pieces draw from traditional Japanese modes and sounds—like the *koto*, an elegant 13-stringed instrument, and *gagaku*, ancient Japanese court music— along with more modern functional harmonies.

The pieces may be performed as a set, or as individual pieces.

Naoko Ikeda

RAFT OF FLOWERS
Hana-Ikada

In the cool spring breeze, imagine cherry blossom petals fluttering silently down onto the surface of a flowing river, and forming a beautiful raft.

PLUM BLOSSOMS
Kobai-Hakubai

Plum blossoms bloom in red and white (and sometimes pink). The photogenic flower is used in many traditional East Asian paintings. Envision this piece as a dance. First, the red blossoms sway gently. The white blossoms imitate in measure 9, and the two gradually entwine as a pair.

PEONIES
Shakuyaku

In Japanese culture, it is customary to liken beautiful women to flowers such as the sweet-scented peony and elegant lily: strong, yet delicate. Be expressive; the melody is important. This piece was also inspired by the painting *Peonies and Butterflies* by Ito Jakuchu (1716–1800).

AOI
Japanese Festival

The Hollyhock Festival (or *Aoi Matsuri*) is one of Japan's major festivals. The hollyhock (*aoi*) leaves and flowers are used to decorate the horse-drawn carriages, period costumes, religious shrines, and other festival ornaments. However, the piece is not only about *Aoi Matsuri*, but also the other wonderful festivals celebrated throughout the year.

SOFT RAIN
Azisai

The rainy season in June is called *tsuyu*. The hydrangeas (*azisai*) are particularly beautiful—and peaceful—after the rain. You will hear Japanese traditional scales in the melody mixed in with modern harmonies. Play with a graceful, delicate touch.

Raft of Flowers
(Hana-Ikada)

Naoko Ikeda

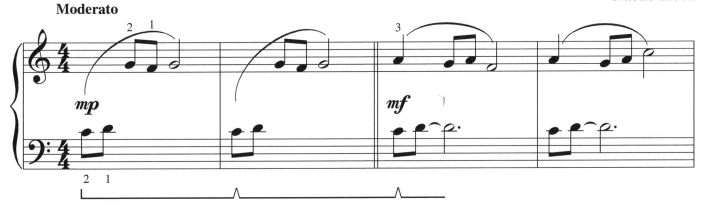

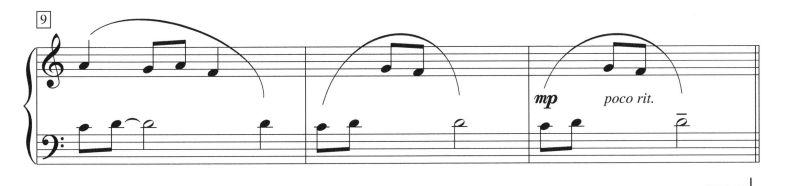

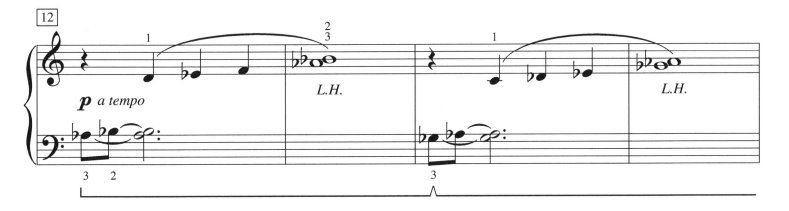

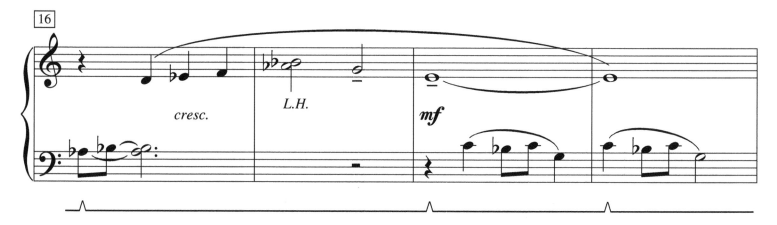

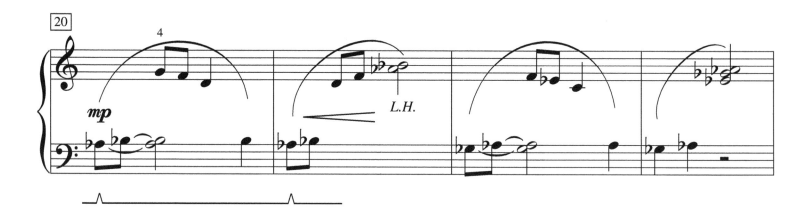

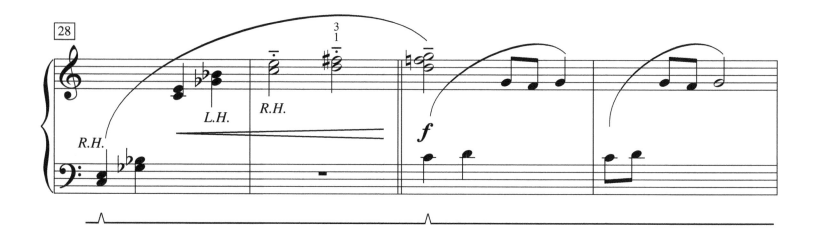

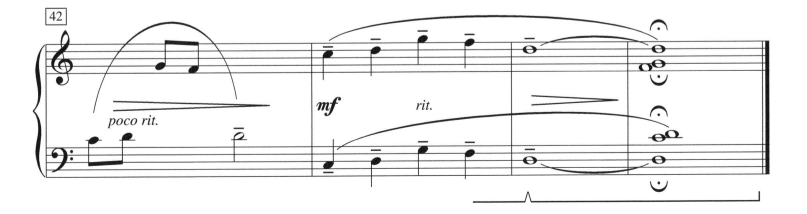

Plum Blossoms
(Kobai-Hakubai)

Naoko Ikeda

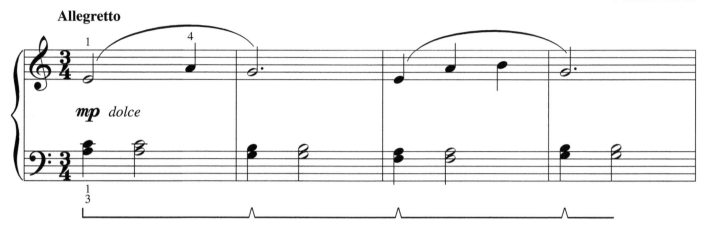

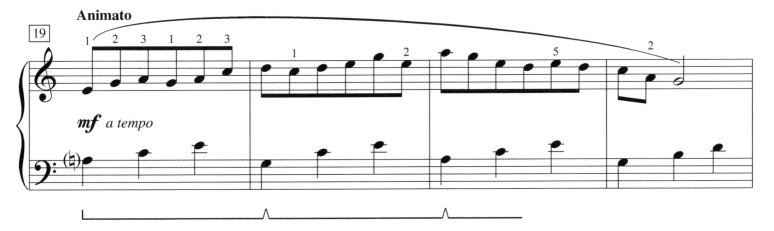

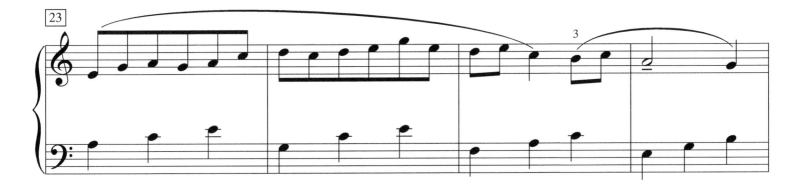

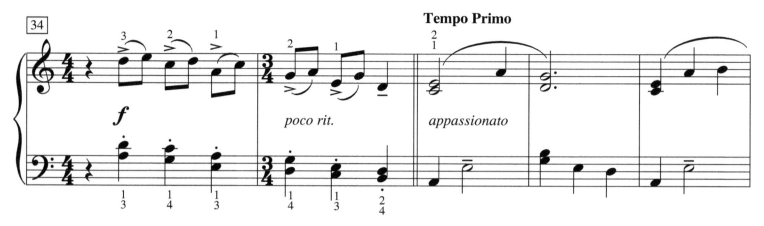

Tempo Primo

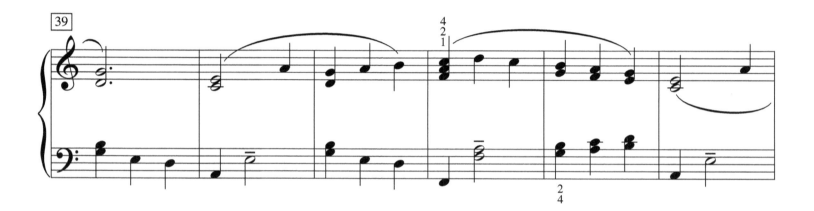

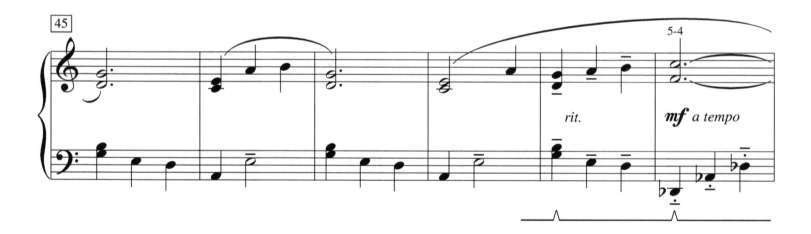

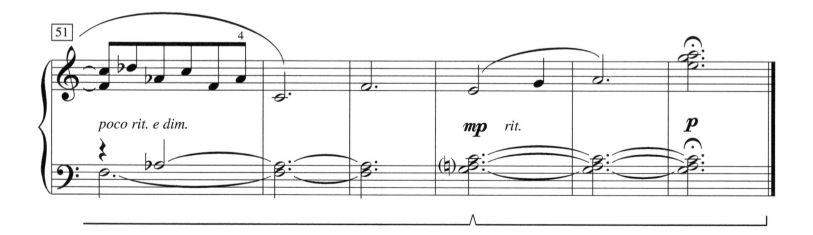

For Mika Goto

Peonies
(Shakuyaku)

Naoko Ikeda

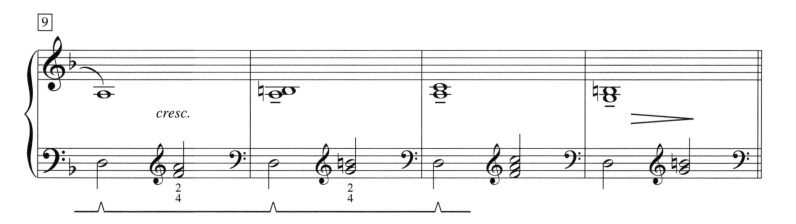

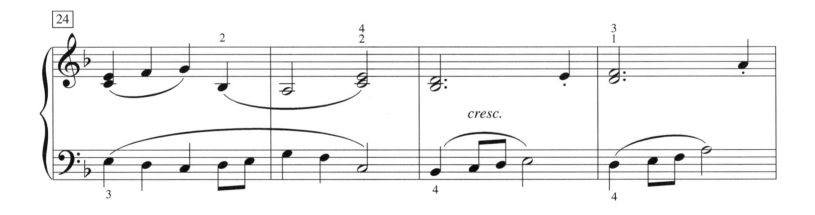

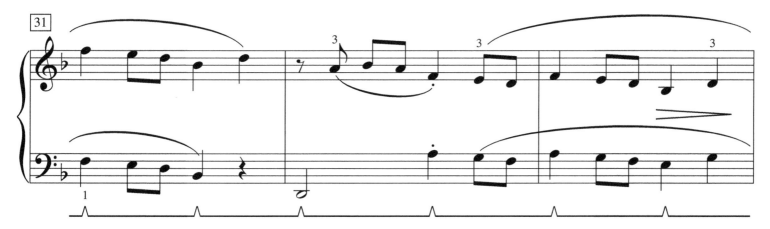

Aoi
(Japanese Festival)

Naoko Ikeda

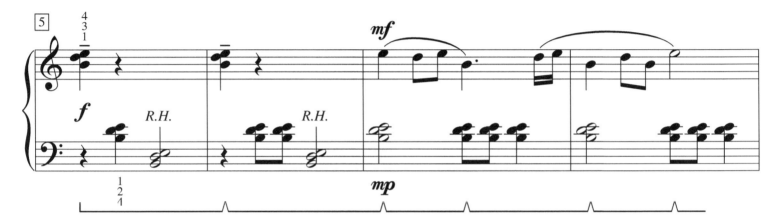

aoi = hollyhocks

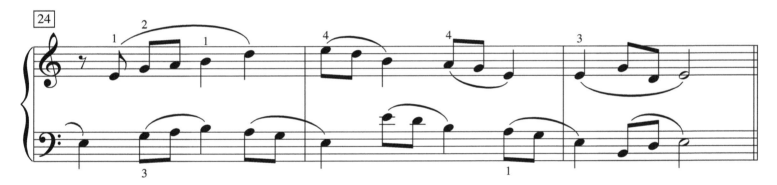

Soft Rain
(Azisai)

Naoko Ikeda

Andantino gentile

azisai = hydrangeas

BIOGRAPHY

Naoko Ikeda lives in Sapporo, Hokkaido in northern Japan. Influenced by classical music, jazz and pop, as well as the piano works of William Gillock, her own music reflects her diverse tastes with beauty, elegance, and humor. Ms. Ikeda is a proud graduate of the Hokusei Gakuen school system, and holds a piano performance degree from Yamaguchi College of Arts. She currently maintains an energetic schedule as both teacher and composer.